Contents

GONE TOO SOON BUT NEVER FORGOTTEN

Gone Too Soon But Never Forgotten

AUTOBIOGRAPHY

Nichelle Rolfe

Djs legacy incorporated

The journey of loss and healing is ongoing, but I am stronger today because of the loved ones I have lost. Their memories encourage me to live fully and with purpose. "Gone Too Soon, Never Forgotten" is my tribute to them and a reminder that, even in the hardest of times, we can find the strength to carry on.

To those reading, may you find hope in these pages. Know that no matter what life throws at you, faith and resilience can carry you through. Hold onto the memories of those you've lost, and let them inspire you to live with purpose and love

Nichelle Rolfe

1

Childhood and Early Losses

Growing up, I faced numerous challenges and hardships. My family was my foundation, and reconnecting with them as an adult was a blessing. But soon after, I started to lose them one by one. Losing my mother and siblings shattered me, each loss more painful than the last. This chapter details those early days, my childhood memories, and the beginnings of the journey that would shape my life.

2

A Heart Broken, Yet Healing

The passing of my mother was a blow I struggled to overcome. She was the one who brought me into this world, and losing her left a void. After her passing, I faced anger, depression, and a sense of abandonment. Yet, through my faith, I found a path toward healing. I began to realize that though she was gone too soon, her love and guidance would remain with me forever.

3

Faith as My Anchor

In times of deep sorrow, I turned to my faith as a source of strength. Jeremiah 29:11 became a guiding scripture for me: "For I know the plans I have for you, declares the Lord, plans to prosper you and not to harm you, plans to give you hope and a future." My faith reminded me that, despite the losses, my life had purpose and that those who had left were never truly forgotten.

4

Loss After Loss, A Test of Strength

The tragedies continued as I lost a nephew to suicide, another to gun violence, and other family members to various circumstances. Each loss was another test, pushing me to find strength within myself to carry on. In this chapter, I recount the grief and how these losses transformed me, making me stronger and more resilient.

5

My Mother's legacy

The legacy of my mother lives on within me. Her love, wisdom, and strength guide me daily. Although she is no longer here, I honor her by living a life she would be proud of. I also feel responsible for carrying on her legacy and sharing her impact on my life.

6

Becoming The Family Anchor

With so many family members gone, I took on a new role as the family matriarch. This chapter discusses the responsibility I feel to be a role model for the next generation, to show them the strength and resilience that has defined our family for generations.

7

Faith Beyond Trials

Life continued to test my faith and resilience. I clung to God's promise and took comfort in knowing that each of my loved ones was in a better place. Through prayer and reflection, I found peace in knowing that, even if they were gone too soon, they would never be forgotten.